The Gates of Light

James Aitchison

The Gates of Light

The Gates of Light
published in the United Kingdom in 2016

by Mica Press
c/o Leslie Bell 47 Belle Vue Road, Wivenhoe, Colchester, Essex
CO7 9LD
www.micapress.co.uk | books@micapress.co.uk

ISBN 978-1-869848-07-1
First Edition 2016.

Copyright © James Aitchison 2016

The right of James Aitchison to be identified as the author of this work has been asserted by him in accordance with the Copyright, Designs and Patents Act of 1988.
All rights reserved.

Acknowledgements:

Since the publication of Foraging: New and Selected Poems in 2009 James Aitchison's poems have appeared in these and other journals:

Acumen, Assent, Awen, Chanticleer Magazine, Coffee House Magazine, Decanto, Earth Love, The French Literary Review, The Frogmore Papers, The Green Queen, The Herald, Krax, The London Magazine, New Writing Scotland, Northwords Now, Painted, spoken, Poetry Church, Poetry Ireland Review, Poetry Review, Poetry Salzburg Review (Spring 2016), Poetry Scotland, Poetry Wales, Quantum Leap, Red Poets, The Rialto, The Scottish Review, The SHOp, Smiths Knoll, The Spectator.

for Norma,
who creates the space in which I write.

Contents

The Year Begins	1
Sitka Hectares	2
Oak	3
Rowan	4
Holly	5
Greys	6
In the Bay of Gibraltar	8
Whaling	9
Weathering	10
Advent Calendar	11
Odds Against Snow	12
Snares	13
Pheasants and Other Words	14
Men don't send each other birthday cards	16
Little People	17
Girl as in ...	18
Tracy's on suicide watch	19
Cold Calling	20
Owning	21
Bottle	22
Falling	23
On the Way to the River	25
Estate	26
Blackout	27
Fire Cans	28
Apart	29
Signature	30
I Remember Tin-bath Wallace Street	31
Wallace Street	32
The Trench	33
At the Church of the Spilled Blood, St Petersburg on Russia Day, 12 June 2012	34
Zoom in: Zoom out	36
Feeding Grounds	37
Good News	38
A Fit Country for Heroes	39
Smog	41
Riveting	42

Analogue	43
The Long Way Round	44
A Gap	45
I Know a Man	46
Reflux	47
Making It Up	48
Light Years	49
Homer, Shakespeare and the Satellites	50
Underworlds	51
Heads	52
Breathing	53
Listen	54
Dream Time	55
Reasons for Wanting Out	56
Extra Time	57
Plan B	58
To Be a Pilgrim	59
Holiday Inn	60
You Are Here	61
Rootstocks	62
Eclipse	63
Seasons	64
Winter's Tales	65
Winter Lines	66
Stubble Fields	67
Sightings	68
On Stirling Bridge	69
On a Minor Road	70
Rough Gardening	71
Carseland Diary	72
Anthem	74
Orchard	75
Passwords	76
Orbit	77
Motorway	78
Husbandries	79
Winter Wrens	80

All night the dreadless angel, unpursued,
Through heaven's wide champain held his way; till Morn
Waked by the circling hours, with rosy hand
Unbarred the gates of light.

Milton *Paradise Lost*, Book VI, lines 1-4

The Year Begins

We slit the throat of a singing bird:
the scalpel finds the syrinx but not the song.

Around the middle of February
my north-world tilts towards the morning light.
A mistle thrush sings. The year begins.

My ear's new batteries
engorge the music of thrush, blackbird and wren.
Birdsong's more startling than poetry.

The year begins again in May
with swifts' wide-gaping shriek
and swallows' reiterative twittering.

When no birds call and migrations fail
insects will inherit the world.

A swift-scream in my head
is more astonishing than headline news.

Sitka Hectares
for Susan Marriott

Take ten paces into a plantation:
rain could be falling and you wouldn't know.
Beneath the canopy the ground is tinder dry.

Far from their Alaskan origins
Sitkas are rampant in these temperate latitudes.

Trunks are charcoal black.
There's a softer blackness between each trunk
but they grow so close they have no surrounding space;
they stand in the way of trees that stand among trees.

No wind can infiltrate; the only stirrings are gaps
in your cortices for movement, sound and light.

Foresters are felling at the edge.
Darkness swallows your cries
and the whining of chainsaws.

People could be searching,
calling your name, your name and you wouldn't know.

Oak

The oak cast shadows and November leaves
across three boundaries:
a sandstone wall, a brick wall and a mixed hedge.

In leaf or skeletal it was a shapely tree.

A chainsaw man worked downwards from the crown,
cutting the heaviest branches to a length
that filled the short-bed lorry twice with logs.

Two men fed branches thicker than my arms
into a snarling, goose-necked harvester
that shredded three loads of chips and bark and brash.

The oak tree was mature before I was born.
It might have outlived me for centuries.

Rowan

We knew it had to go. We'd known for years.
The Kashmir rowan
grew faster than our three native rowan trees
in the softer climate of the Carse.

Kill another shapely tree?
Its late white berries were the waxwings' choice.
Leaves choked the gutters. Gutters' overflow
streaked the whitewashed walls.
What if – a six-year-long what if –
its roots reached the foundations of the house?

The Kashmir rowan tree wasn't big enough
for the three-man team
who dismembered the mature oak tree last year.
Another year? It might be too big for me.

I knew how it could be done;
I didn't know if I could do what I knew.

My twelve-foot wooden ladder was long enough
but its shafts were too wide for the upper trunk
and too narrow
to span the trunk and a branch that would take my weight.

Propped against roundness, the top rung was askew.
I climbed in shuffle-footsteps:
left foot, and then left-and-right on the same rung.

I used a handsaw.
I burned out two Black & Decker saws
felling small cypresses in Gloucestershire.

I roped the branch I was sawing to a thicker branch.
When I'd sawn through

I climbed down, loosened the rope and lowered the branch.
I roped the last branch to the trunk.

The heartwood was tight-ringed;
the dense weight of the trunk trapped the saw blade.
When I'd pulled it free
I bought another Black & Decker saw.

A watercolour waxwing in my room
pecks red berries from a native tree.

Holly

Blackbirds eat the berries and excrete the seeds.
Seeds germinate in bird-shit-fertile soil.
When the holly seedlings are sapling-high
we heel them in between the parent plants
and elder, hazel, beech in the mixed hedge.
Hazel and beech – we cut them back again
last month; they were reaching to be trees.
Holly grows slowly; its trunk-age rings are tight.
This year's saplings won't need cutting back in my lifetime.
Leaves glisten all year round in a green light.

Greys

From August to April I couldn't read or write
in that dislocated interim.
I was a displaced person, an immigrant,
when we retired from Stirling to Cheltenham.
To be adaptable – I'm an old grey man –
you need an opportune intelligence.

I sensed it just before the furred grey blur
became a squirrel
stop-startling, eyeing, twitching, scurrying
along our undulating fence.
Our garden's ornamental boundary
spanned the gap in the squirrels' corridor
of chestnut trees on town's-edge Hill Court Road
and bridged the gap between squirrels' world and mine.

In the south in late spring every year
we weeded out new shoots
sprung from autumn nuts the greys had cached.
The seedlings might have made a chestnut grove
if we had left them to grow.

Winter months were seldom mild enough
in Scotland for buried chestnuts to take root.

In Cheltenham we watched grey squirrels perform
the kind of aero-acrobatic games
we'd seen them play
in Stirling gardens, parks and tree-lined streets,
places they'd colonised so long ago
that they had native rights of residence
in their semi-natural habitats.

Back in Scotland now
I read reports of a national campaign

to save red squirrels, the indigenous breed,
by weeding out the alien immigrant greys.

In the Bay of Gibraltar

In water and air
dolphins are elemental acrobats.
How did they learn
their fiercely measured choreography?
Pairs and trios and quartets and quintets
leap-arc-dive in perfect unison.

I left the sea a million years ago.

Dolphins know the habits of the boat.
They plunge from port to starboard, starboard to port
and then they soar
so high above the level of the deck
that for a moment we see eye-to-eye.

Whaling

We took no photographs when we went whale-hunting
from Provincetown, Massachusetts in the fall.
We boarded the ocean-going launch without a camera.
Memory selects what's memorable.

I don't know how to judge seas' distances:
the Pilgrim Monument was matchstick-size.
The engine idled.
The launch yawed on the Atlantic humpback swell.

The lookout yelled. A sighting. The engine roared
and the prow rose high above the gurling wake.

Minutes? Seconds? Sea-time is different.
The throttled-down engine purred, 'Meat, blubber, bone.'

The lookout called, 'Port side. Two hundred yards.'
Passengers aimed their cameras for the shoot.
I saw no whales.

I raised a hand to screen the October sun:
an exhalation from a sleek black wave
was an audible rainbow, a whale's fountain-breath.

Flukes carved an elemental arc
and sank – bone, blubber, ambergris, cat-food –
a colossal act of unhuman ponderous grace
in the slow-motion real time of the sea.

Weathering

The beating engine and the quavering hull
lullaby me through the Sound of Mull.

And sailing north, I follow a rainbow
in the bow-wave of MV Hamnavoe.

I walk in sun-struck snow. Snow disappears
in the blind eyelash rainbow of my tears.

Snowflakes fall, dissolve and overnight
they freeze again as needle-points of light.

Hoar-frost thickens plant cells' cellulose
and furs the petals of a Christmas rose.

From these improbable realities
come plausible impossibilities.

My shoulder-blades are stumps of angel wings.
I croak the song my fallen angel sings.

Advent Calendar

Annunciations appear from thin air:

a hush of falling snow on fallen snow

gold and purple crocuses
after the hardest winter for thirty years

an aftertaste of grief
in the perfume of a kitchen hyacinth

a fluting blackbird, a staccato thrush
a hreeing ecstasy of swifts
green-lemon May leaves rinsed with liquid light

birds on Republic of Ireland postage stamps
bringing singing for more than forty years
poems from Robert Nye in County Cork

a drum-roll of a million single beats –
sweet thunder of The Dream in Gloucestershire –
of hailstones on a conservatory roof

the tight-grained density
of heartwood holly, laburnum, elder, oak

white filaments beneath the translucent skin
of a ripe gooseberry.

An advent calendar lasts the whole year long.

Odds Against Snow
for F M M MacLeod

Bookmakers offer odds against a fall
of snow on London rooftops on Christmas Day.

Children wish for days and nights of snow:
a garden under snow is a wish-made world
and a child who makes first footprints on a lawn
walks into a mythology of snow.

Bookmakers know big cities overheat
even in midwinter.
In betting shops, post offices and banks,
in branches of M & S and Waterstone's
the staff wear summer shirts the whole year round.

A child is rolling a snowball.
When it's a wheel she turns it to make a sphere,
a wheel, a sphere, a wheel, a turning sphere
until it's too heavy for her to move.

Cold is gnawing through the child's gloves.
The sphere asks her for a second, smaller sphere
but she feels her fingers swollen with frozen blood.
Burning, not freezing. The pain's unbearable.

She goes indoors. She weeps
at the scalding agony of thawing snow
as blood flows back into her fingertips.

London's thermals penetrate the clouds.
Snow above London falls as sleet or rain.

Snares
for Maggie Butt

A bird by Edward Thomas or John Clare
is clearer than a sighting in the field.

Even migrating birds are penned and sealed
in evergreen black foliage,
but it is the bird that sets the snare,
fastening the poet to the page.

Clare's Mary-craziness could not be healed
by the birds he heard.
Thomas was distracted from despair
by the 'La-la-la' of his unknown bird.

A poem by Clare or Thomas is a cage
that's open to the air.

A bird by Clare or Thomas is a prayer.

Birdsong is music poets can't record
and yet their birds are preternaturally real
when I hear them on the thoroughfare
of the printed word.

Pheasants and Other Words

We brake and stop
more startled than the iridescent cock pheasant
somnambulating along a Z-bend country road.
We're close enough
to see the dark-bar feathers of its trailing brown tail.
When its brain acknowledges the car
the pheasant walks faster before it flies away.
It flies as if it's still learning how to fly.

Some metaphors sound better when they're mixed.

Words don't break cover when I try to flush them out.
My brain's dendritic thickets are thinner now
but the huddled words – Do they know I'm hunting them? –
have found an overgrown hide in the undergrowth.

To find the word I mutter other words
with similar meanings, similar syllables and sounds –
necromancy ... pharmacy ... *alchemy*.
This isomorphic wordplay is my only way –
armada ... regatta ... *flotilla* – of calling them out
to find the word among words on the tip of my tongue –
Einstein... Eisenstein ... Rogers and *Hammerstein*.

Gutting a pheasant in an abandoned poem
I found a wad of farmed lentils in its crop,
not freely foraged insects and wild seeds.
I found black-purple pockmarks where pellets had struck.
Gutting was easier than I'd feared: pheasants are bred for it.

Fool that I am!
(The '!' is an old man's groan and a pheasant's squawk.)
Five lines back, a day-and-night mind ago I thought
if I found words to fit persons, actions and birds
I'd own not only their names but their thisnesses.

I must have known and yet it's only now
nearing the end that I know I'll never know how
to catch a pheasant in a paraphrase.

Similarities of sense and sound?
The pheasant has flown away but I hear 'hukuck-hukuff',
the hiccough call of the disembodied bird.
The call's cut off when we start the car again.

Men don't send each other birthday cards

Men don't send each other birthday cards.
It doesn't occur to us to give our date
of birth: there's nothing much to celebrate.

We might end a letter 'With kind regards'
but never with a little cross like this:
x. Men don't understand that kind of kiss.

'Gorgeous', 'poignant', 'mammogram' are words
too feminine for men to feel or say.
A woman weeps on her daughter's wedding day.

A man goes bird-watching; a woman guards
her firebird's ashes and the sacrament.
A man keeps up his prick of discontent.

A woman hears the melody and chords.
A man hears drum-beats and a booming bass.
A woman sobs into her pillow-case.

Little People

Little people have no lineage
before the census of 1801.
They pay the maintenance of palaces
and heritable realms; the title deeds
are held by kings and queens and heads of state.

Little people have no history.
The Times, The Guardian, The Daily Telegraph
never publish the obituaries
of little people. Little people pay
for parents' death-notes in the local press.

The genome that begins with African Eve –
the short-lived prehistoric matriarch
of our deviant chromosomes
and wordless mother of all languages –
Eve's genome lives in everyone on earth.

As Eve's descendants, little people share
the same heredity as kings and queens:
an irreversible entitlement
to majesty and commonality.
Rich need little people to know they're rich.
Kings and queens need little people to rule.

Girl as in ...

A waitress in the Golden Lion Hotel,
a check-out girl at Greenyards nursery,
a tobacco-counter girl in Sainsbury's
have laminated names on their uniforms.

Girl as in 'I'm a Tuesday-to-Friday girl.'
Girl as in 'My mum looks after Sam.'
Girl as in 'What I'd really, really like
is stub my cigarette in his eye.'

Girl as in how it might-have-should-have-been
before she signed for the minimum hourly rate.

Her Tuesdays-to-Fridays are an afterwards.

I thank the woman by name as if I knew
who she is in her other part-time life.

You're welcome,' the woman says. 'Have a nice day.'

'Thanks again, Elaine-Fiona-Clare,'
I say as I remove my Mastercard.

'Thank you.' A girlish 'Bye-ee.' And 'Take care.'

Tracy's on suicide watch

Tracy's on suicide watch in Cornton Vale.
She stole a pair of shoes, her second offence.

Money-laundering protection racketeers
in banks and finance establishments,
fraudsters in conglomerates,
oligarchs in energy cartels
have chums in Westminster.

'Pneumonia' and 'Cardiac Arrest'
on the certificates
could mean hunger and hypothermia.

'Cash for honours? What's the going rate?
It's politic to have a lord on board.'

Tracy's children were taken into care.
They might be safer sleeping on the street.

Davy, Mick and Jack – these three wee men
were honourable commoners.
Now they're arsed in scarlet, peers of the realm.

Cold Calling

When they came cold-calling at my door
I used to say to the Yahweh Holy pair
'I have a faith. It serves me well.
Thank you for calling,' I used to say. 'Goodbye.'

I make a faith from days' realities
and mind's default: a garden, poems and you.

Now when the bell rings and I open the door
and find two Yahweh Holies on the step
I shout abuse. In fact, I lower my voice
but a whispered curse can sound as loud as a scream.

Do they come calling to save my soul
or am I part of their quota for the day?

I live as quietly as I can;
contentment is despair wrapped up in love.
But when the Holies called again last week
I told them to bugger off.

Anger to hide my fear? And arrogance
to mask inadequacy? I know. I know.

Even if the condition I call faith
is just a set of inconsolable genes
I'll still tell Yahweh's Holies to bugger off.

Owning

Sightings –
I don't know what they are until I learn their names.
Not Latin binomials, just plain English words.

I check the guide:
The balls of diving fluff
I saw from the footbridge over the River Forth
were my first sightings of Little Grebes.

And rivers –
in this narrow land I should know the names
of rivers that reach the sea
and the names of their tributaries.

I check the map:
the River Ericht and the River Earn.
Knowing's a duty and a legacy;
I own the open secret of their names.

And someone –
he was in the news but I forget his name,
a lord, duke, earl or chieftain of some clan –
says he owns the Cuillin Hills on Skye.

Bottle

Doors bursting open slamming slamming shut
red wine dripping down the dining-room wall
a wedding-gift cafetière in razor shards
on the kitchen floor
screaming silences cramped sofa nights.

Forever was foreplay. This was afterwards.

He was in the kitchen, drinking, when I got back.
I didn't say, 'If only for your liver's sake.'
I remember what I said:
'I'll unpack the shopping and then get lunch.'

He smashed his empty glass on the tiled floor.

A spasm of rage as quick as a flicked switch –
Not rage. No. Not hatred. I don't know what.
A power surge.
The certainty was irresistible.

A two-litre plastic bottle of lemonade.
He had his back to me. The bottle struck.
I staggered at the impact. He stood still.
The bottle struck again.
The solid thud of his head on the kitchen floor
was the last sound he made.

There was no blood.
There might have been a hair or a trace of sweat;
I wiped the bottle clean
but left my Waitrose fingerprints on its neck.

I put the bottle back in the shopping bag
and then I called for an ambulance.

Falling

After Browning

He hears a buzzing somewhere in his brain.
The noise might be the onset of migraine.
He knows that he is falling in love again.

Yes, he's in love again, and lovers feel
that loving is an exquisite ordeal:
magical, irrational and real.

His fall was sudden, heedless and so deep
he started smoking again and losing sleep.
The secret was too clamorous to keep.

He feels love's throbbing neural networks swell
like that arousing whatsit by Ravel.
He has to tell her. Tomorrow? He must tell.

'You love me? I believe that you believe.
I smell it in your scented aftershave;
I hear it in your quavering recitative.

'Forever? No That's too long to stay true.
How will you love me when your love falls through
and you fall out of love, as lovers do?'

'Fall through? Fall out? But how? I mean …I thought
you felt the same as me.' Love's taut slip-knot
grows tighter round his heart and round his throat.

'Love is like an extrasensory sense.
Fever-brained, a lover has no defence
against love's all-or-nothing innocence.'

He's hot. He sweats. How can she be so cold?
He shakes. He shivers. She's so self-controlled.
Bitch! Whore! She has him in love's stranglehold.

His innocence? She means virginity.
And she ... Love-knot. Slip-knot. He loosens his tie
and twists it round her neck, choking her cry.

He watches himself watching the woman die.

On the Way to the River

I was too young to listen with intent
to the river singing on its shingle bed.
I didn't hear the song implant its sound
but I knew its music when I went back again.

On the way to the river
my prickling scalp and the earth's unsteadiness
proved the nearness of the beast
watching me from a cave among the rocks.

I was aged seven or eight:
I knew the beast was unsayable;
I knew I was too old to hold your hand.

You said, 'Wild garlic.' You said, 'Marsh marigolds.'
And when you said, 'These are hazel trees,'
the thicket and the name eclipsed the sun.

My nameless beast,
your naming of flowers and trees
and the river making music visible
gave my boyhood a pagan holiness.

My mind was smaller than my feral brain.

You were too ill to say, 'Goodbye.'
On clouded, moonless, starless nights I wept
and in the dark I reached out for your hand.

Estate

I couldn't find them when we cleared the house –
his birth, marriage or death certificates.
And he was too young to have made a will.
A will? He had no money, no property.

When he died sixty-five years ago
a bit of my boyhood brain was cauterized.

In a last sifting of family photographs
I found him smiling at me in black and white.
He's sitting with workmates at the open door
of a cabin in a logging camp
somewhere in 1930s' Canada.

Sixty-five years. Our lives seem far apart.
I write a poem; my father fells a tree.

But I have his genes. I inherit his estate.
By the time he died he had made his mind
in mine a dangerous, legendary place.

I'm writing this to certify his life.
I'll print out a hard copy of these lines.

He looks invulnerable in the photograph.

Blackout

Coal-gas street lamps were never lit.
There was more shining from a crescent moon
than from all the blindfold houses in the town.

The only telephone in our neighbourhood
of two-room, jerry-built slum tenements
was in the corner shop
at the junction of Thornhill Road and Wallace Street.

No one owned a car;
petrol coupons were foreign currency.
And ration books were Biblical:
'Lose your ration book and you'll starve to death.'

When the Clydesdales disappeared from the brewery
the rumour was butcher meat.
The horses were at work on nearby farms.

Our fathers were away for years and years;
we trampled the allotments to hardpan.

There were more stars in the night sky
than sequins on Anna Neagle's evening gowns.

Fire Cans

When we had nothing left to burn
or when our mothers called us from the dark –
first name and surname:
Tam Bryce, Jack Kerr, Billy Tait, Dave Henderson –
we whirled our fire cans round and round and round
and then let go ...

A clattering tin
is scattering the ash from fallen stars
across the black back-court at Wallace Street.

Apart

Our two-apartment homes in the tenements
were planned to keep the proletariat –
foundry workers and their families –
apart from the foundry owners.
I grew up in an apartheid state.

I went away while I was still at home
and lost the curiosity and dread,
the instinctual, brain-stem, nerve-end faculty
that had kept the feral boy alive.

My voice – mock-Third Programme BBC –
falsifies my origins.
If you ask me where or when I say
'I was a foundling' or 'My parents were so poor
they couldn't afford to have me until I was ten.'

The facts of my childhood are commonplace
and mythological.
Even if denial is my defence
against poverty, my phoney voice
and smart-arse humourless jokes corrupt the myth.

Signature

I was a child; I couldn't read or write.
My parents said I had to sign my name.
My father had a dry-ink Biro pen.
He wrote, James Aitchison, his name and mine,
handed the pen to me
and said I had to copy his signature.

I tried. I knew the task was serious.
A child can sense his parents' anxieties
in eyes that look at you and then look away,
and in a tone of voice:
'Take your time' meant time was running out.

I practised. But a small child can't portray
adults' alien realities.
The marks I made were not a signature:
James Aitchison meant someone, something more.

I practised until a teller in a bank
or post office – the place where money hid –
agreed the squiggle, James Aitchison, was me.

Seventy years of practising my name –
I open and close accounts with the flick of a pen –
have made my name illegible again.

I Remember Tin-bath Wallace Street

I remember tin-bath Wallace Street
and the back-court, brick-built communal latrine.
('Tin-bath?', 'Back-court?' Yes. I hear what you say.)
Now – a bathroom and four bedrooms, two en-suite.

Sixty-six years ago is yesterday.

My free school dinners were bought with my father's life.
I remember gagging on gristly meat.

He made music on the mandolin.
The music stopped. I never heard him play.
Aged ten, I hadn't mind enough for grief.

My mother lived until she was ninety-nine.
I write too late the words I didn't say:
'My loving leveller. My plebeian queen.'

I write another line and I betray
the scapegoat innocence of poverty.
I didn't know we hadn't the means to choose
our whereabouts then. I choose now. I can pay.

Their brief long lives were – are – truer than mine.
A poet is a fickle go-between.

And now I've lived so long I repeat, repeat ...
Too long to long for an eternity.

I remember hand-me-down Clark's shoes.
Now – I've more pairs than I'll ever use.

Wallace Street

'Wear your school blazer, school tie and white shirt,
speak properly and nobody will guess
246 Wallace Street was your first address.
Not that there's anything wrong in good clean dirt.'

When I left my parents' You Are Here
I added colour to their pencil maps,
filled in their local, vocal, social gaps
with adolescent arrogance and fear.

I write another line, another page.
I know my mapmaking will never match
the plain truth of my parents' pencil sketch.
And now I'm almost twice my father's age.

The Trench

No need for shoring up with beams and props:
the soil is one part loam to three parts clay.
The walls of the new trench will not collapse.

Men and boys with long-shaft shovels delve
more than shaft-deep, more than their body weight.
The diggers are aged seventy to twelve.

Guards see the diggers as male but not mankind;
they'll have no reason to deny this day
or keep tight-shut compartments in their minds.

The guards examine their Kalashnikovs.
They're growing impatient, afraid they'll miss their turn:
young girls are screaming in the olive groves.

At the Church of the Spilled Blood, St Petersburg on Russia Day, 12 June 2012

'The view of the Church from Nevsky Prospekt is absolutely breath-taking.'

I gasped for breath to keep pace with the guide.

Inside the Church
the floor-to-ceiling iconographies
of bleeding saints
and God's anointed genealogy
of godson Romanovs
were too proclamatory to be true.
I was baptized into austerity.

I left the Church.
Outside, I struck a match; smoke caught my breath.

Their uniform tunics were a size too big,
their faces too small
beneath their round-rimmed Soviet-style peaked caps.
They stood more than an outstretched arm apart
between Konyushennaya Place
and the east bank of Griboyedova Canal.

The boys were too young
even for a glasnost Komsomol,
too young, too few to block the protest march.

Protest? I saw no banners, heard no chants.
The column was a family promenade
along the far side of the canal.
Smaller children clung to white balloons.
If the children let go
balloons would soar like a great flock of plump doves.

Some of the strolling boys were as old, as young
as the boys in uniform.

We couldn't stay.
To reach the Moyka River water-bus
we had to cross the cordon.
I'm short; the nearest boy was shorter still
with tunic sleeves down to his fingertips.

Around a corner – my city-centre map
or my memory has lost a street –
a long line of army trucks
and hundreds of men in summer battledress.

Zoom in: Zoom out

Zoom in and you magnify the flies
feeding on the tears in children's eyes.

> Save the Children, Médecins Sans Frontières
> pay warlords, presidents and premiers.

Child-skin is tight as cling-film round their bones;
their rib cages are little xylophones.

> Oxfam – Oxford Committee for Famine Relief –
> bring crates of bottled water for the chief.

Other children's bellies swell: a glut
of kwashiorkor fluid in the gut.

> Christian Aid, Red Crescent and Red Cross
> might as well be making candy floss.

The least sick children who meet the movie star
have never been inside a cinema.

How many? God knows. No one keeps a list.
Zoom out. And out. The children don't exist.

Feeding Grounds

I was a member of M.C.F.A. –
the Movement for Colonial Freedom in Africa.
I collected signatures. I marched.
I knew my undergraduate righteousness
would free the continent.

Labourers could be harvesting beans or maize
from the irrigated fields.
They're growing roses for St Valentine
and grapes for Pinotage.

There was clean drinking water last month.
No one saw the men who came by day
and took away the purifying machine.

Infants with big unblinking sightless eyes
and bulging bellies
have thinner skin, fewer sinews, softer bones.

Hyenas scrape the soil from shallow graves.
Swallows in their African feeding grounds
eat blowflies rising from scraps of putrid flesh.

Good News

The headlines in my head tonight – good news –
are beamed down from a February moon
above the Carse of Forth.

The moon is clearer now
than all the televised ills of Africa.

A new mass grave?
Or is it last year's footage? A repeat?
The latest U. N. concentration camp
for refugees looks like the last, the next.

Television reporters and camera crews –
What do they eat and drink? Where do they sleep?
They should all go home.

We can do nothing more for Africa.
Our mother, African Eve, ate her afterbirth.

I sent another cheque this afternoon.
Tonight I watch the passage of the moon.

A Fit Country for Heroes
for William Paxton

'What is our task? To make Britain a fit country for heroes to live in.'
David Lloyd George

I've never been to war. I've never killed.
These unimaginable lines are willed.

The numbers die-stamped on the discs they wore
on cords around their necks in the Great War
were checked against the regimental roll
for dead men's names. Some of the dead were whole.

When body-parts were scattered, searchers matched
a torso, arms and legs with a detached
head. Bodies harvested in no-man's-land
or where the killing had been hand-to-hand
were indistinguishable unless a shred –
khaki or grey – identified the dead.

If not, parts of a comrade were interred
with an enemy. The graves are shared.

* * *

In days they grew familiar with the stench
of shit and cordite in their front-line trench.

Trenches and shell craters have been filled;
the lunar landscape is a level field.
Over the named and nameless, white headstones
rise from a hundred thousand skeletons.
The grass is close-cut as a bowling green.

Men died by telegram, shrapnel and phosgene,
machine-gun fire and shell-shock cowardice
until the moment of the armistice.

Ceasefire. My grandfather was shipped home
to two rooms in a patriotic slum
tenement that had been jerry-built.

Lloyd George knew nothing of survivors' guilt.

Smog

Unless they came from beyond the back of beyond –
the Mull of Galloway or the Western Isles –
students lived at home and travelled in.

Smog thickened as I walked down Gilmorehill
till I couldn't see the other side of the street.
Lights were so dim I cast no shadows on the pavement.

Tramcars were late, or lost.
Some had turned back and were berthed in their depots.
The few that passed me sounded far away.

In the city centre there was light enough
to see black particles floating in the fog
and black mucus on my handkerchief.

Outside Buchanan Street station – trains east and north –
a foghorn cried, 'Times. Evenin Times-ah. Times.'

Me? Yes. At home: white pillows and white sheets,
laundered shirts and clean handkerchiefs.
I knew then I could never repay the debt.

Riveting

On days when air was clarified by frost
and a translucent moon came close to earth
I'd hear the rhythms of pneumatic riveting hammers
in a high-tiered lecture room.

Some of the shipyard men had served their time
when white-hot iron bolts were still slammed home
by sledgehammers with half-width heads,
precision instruments in riveters' hands.

Riveters worked a forty-eight-hour week
ten, twenty, thirty, forty, eighty feet
above the Clyde. They felt the scaffolding
sway like a ship at sea when strong winds blew.

Shipyard credentials? None. My student jobs –
summer gophering on Grangemouth building sites,
delivering Christmas mail –
were so short-term they were paid holidays.

Back in the lecture room, Alexander Scott
taught in a voice that rattled window panes,
electrified the air and woke the dead.
William Dunbar is chanting in my head.

Analogue

The word-processing programme was designed
by a super-intelligent, semi-literate
microelectronic mastermind.

My sweaty flustering was like a fear:
I couldn't format networks in my brain
to match the menus in the strange software.

I couldn't decode the new cryptography.
New? It's a dead or dying language now,
like my schoolboy Latin, physics, chemistry.

Lama, llama, peak, peek, Peke and pique
are passed by Tools/Spellcheck, and cheque and Czech,
and boys, girls, buoys, grilse, Buddha, buddleia, Sikh.

A thousand megabytes are at my fingertips,
or will be if I reprogram my brain
to function like a box of microchips.

Click copy for a short-term memory trace.
Click the next icon, cut – your story's lost
in the infinity of cyberspace.

The Long Way Round

Switching to Microsoft
was learning an alien language in middle age.

Twenty years later
the word processor in my brain
still can't match the program word-for-Word.

And with fewer thoughts to think,
unthinkingly my neural networks shrink.

I make new spelling errors: I fuse twowords,
I miss a letter of the alpabet
and full stops at the ends of sentences

My new Dell keyboard isn't as accurate
as my manual Olivetti's quick brown fox.
My finger-speed keeps time,
geriatric slow, with my speed of thought.

Microsoft shortcuts?
I'm quicker when I take the long way round.

A Gap

A missing word feels like a missing state
of mind. Not absentmindedness: a gap,
a mental void I don't know how to fill,
a here-be-monsters on my neural map.

As a schoolboy I would turn a tap
and spates would spill
from mind to pen to pages of foolscap.

Now? Days and night and years. I can't distil
a sentence from the gap; no art or skill
can open the gates of light. I've made a date
with darkness once again. And so I wait.

I Know a Man

My word processor doesn't have a mind
but it has thoughts I don't know how to think.

I store more memories on microchips
and lose my way in parsing the grammar of time:
the historic present, the future-in-the-past.

This attempt to map a different route
from prelinguistic centres of my brain
will end in artificial intelligence.

Truth isn't lying waiting to be found
out there; I make it up as I go along.

I still send poems to friends I haven't seen
for years. And two new friends I've never met
send me their love. They don't know who I am.

I'd say 'love' in return but I don't trust
my little spasms of generosity.

I ask the reflex questions of old age –
will these things see me out: my lawnmower,
my teeth, my hair, my hearing and my mind?

'I know a man who knows a man who knows
all there is to know about these things.
I'll have a word and then get back to you.'

Reflux

I meet more people in dreams than in waking life
but even in company
it's years since I last blushed or felt the need.
My neural networks for embarrassment
failed so long ago they've silted up.

And yet when I'm alone my petty crimes,
betrayals, blurted gaucheries, bad-taste jokes –
one employer paid me to go away –
come back like a reflux
of acid from my gut into my mouth.

I write more than I speak but can't write off
the raw intransigence of incidents
that won't recast themselves as anecdotes.

My past's a presence that I can't control.
Awake, asleep, my mind is never whole.

Making It Up

I find it easier to write than sleep
some nights until my small-hours' longhand slurs.
Not 'easy': I'm ill-at-ease with ease.

On mornings after the oblivion
of the night before
my glyphs are fuddled, indecipherable.

Bits of language defect, and now my words
no longer fill the word-store in my brain.

I've no deadlines to meet
and yet I wake up knowing I've overslept.
I've no appointments but I'm running late.

I've no idea where these lines will lead.
Not 'lead': I make them up as I go along.

The lines I'm following are following me
through the dwindling neural circuitry
that keeps me in mind.

Light Years

We manufacture light and grow star-blind.

Interplanetary telescopes
find stars and stars beyond the last beyond,
more than the world's astronomers can count.
They trust the virtual reality
of artificial intelligence
to number the new-found stars.

In unlit places –
Orkney, Barra, the Mull of Galloway –
I step outside at night.
I strike a match
and for a moment
the sulphur spurt obscures the stars.

A star must shed its light across light years
before we see it shine.

Match snuffed,
starlight is instantaneous.
And yet its shining
is so long ago, so far away
the stars I see
or planet Earth could be already dead.

Homer, Shakespeare and the Satellites

A big-bang cosmos has no farthermost,
no limitation and no last frontier.
Astrophysicist and engineer
design a space probe with a bigger thrust.

Grounded in galactic wanderlust
and anti-gravity, the volunteers
at NASA are the heirs of charioteers
in Homer's heavenly future-in-the-past.

And literate astronomers have cast
Uranus' moons as women in Shakespeare:
Merchant, Tempest, Othello, Hamlet, Lear.
Rosalind's as you like her: tanned, robust.

Old titanium satellites don't rust
in their xerostatic atmosphere.
Some are transmitting signals we can hear
but cannot understand: the codes are lost.

Homer ... Shakespeare ... Can little poets accost
the heavens? On icy nights the stars appear
so close to planet Earth that I can hear
the crystal chittering of stellar dust.

Underworlds

They painted by the light of tallow lamps,
stone bowls with animal fat and bulrush wicks.

Pigments were madder, ochre, gentian
and blood, with water from the healing well.

Painters made ladders and sistine scaffolding
to reach the ceilings in the deeper caves.

They painted cavernous gloaming underworlds
teeming with the creatures they killed to live.

Auroch, ibex, bison, deer and horse –
lit by the wavering light of little flames
the reborn animals roam across the sky.

Heads

I lay face-down on the trolley
and eased my weight along the passageway.

When I stood up
I saw in the day-time dusk of clouded light
seeping through a gap in the thick-slabbed roof
that I was buried alive inside a mound.

    *   *   *

Seers spoke to the spirits of the place:
massed tribes' levering aligned the megaliths
and raised a hollow hill from level ground.

When the day passed, days passed, and the sun was lost
in mist and leprosy
seers placed severed heads on the solstice stones.

    *   *   *

A needle ... a vein on the back of my left hand ...
The gadolinium in the syringe
went to my head.

I lay on my back on the trolley and slid head-first –
my head was wedged between two book-end pads –
scared stiff into the machine
that scanned magnetised slices of my brain.

I kept my head. I shivered when I stood up.

I took my metal-buckled trouser belt –
I shiver in recurring aftershocks,
bone-marrow millennial shudderings –
my wrist-watch, coins and magnetic credit cards.

Breathing

Sandstone is porous: little pockets of air
between the grains of sand in sandstone walls
are breathing spaces for the dead.

I heard them first in my grandparents' house
through lath-and-plaster from the outer walls.
My grandmother said it was rats;
my grandfather mouthed dead names from the First
World War.
I travelled to university by train.
When it stopped in the tunnel east of Buchanan Street
I inhaled dead men's tubercular breath.
I felt them breathing through my lungs.
And when, all at once, the men inhaled,
the suction started whirlpools in my brain.

Some nights my breathing keeps me awake:
incipient emphysema and permaphlegm
wheeple like a woodwind in my throat.

The oboe tuning up is out of tune;
it sounds like dead men breathing through sandstone walls.

Listen

the four at the next table talk and laugh
louder because the four or are they six
talking laughing at the table next to them
are louder because people at the next ...

no carpets curtains no soft furnishings
to sponge some of the talking laughing noise
the noise is not out there it's in my head

I hear voice noise I can't make out a word
talking laughing howling in my head
louder not a single human word

I lean across the table to hear you speak
I'm surrounded by sounds inside my head
I listen to you as quietly as I can
louder I can't hear louder what you say

Dream Time

Dreams are oracular. No, they don't foretell
my future but they sometimes show me how
I got from there-and-then to here-and-now.

Unthinking afterthoughts, my dreams forecast
what will have been, the future in the past.

The historic present is-was-is a tense
that – 'Shakespeare writes' – can make the past make sense.

And in the tenses of the paradigm
'to be' are many ways of parsing time.

The past's not flashbacked but fastforwarded
by time's word processor in my head.

Nonsense dreams, like poems, are serious play
rehearsing for tomorrow's yesterday.

Between my day and its dream parallel
world there are few differences of fact:
the meaning of a dream is the dreaming act.

Reasons for Wanting Out

When I'm too frail
to tackle dear-life seasonal garden tasks
and last year's oak leaves choke the water-butt;
when there's no humour in my humoresques
and my toenails
grow far away, too far for me to cut
and then too far to see;
when networks shut
and neurotransmitters' trickle turns to drought;
when I can't read the pages on my desk;
when reason fails and I do not know me;
when I'm incapable of doubt;
when memories forget where they should be
I'll write free verse and call it poetry.

Extra Time

Time slows down to match my speed of thought.

When I was juggling balls –
one-and-two-and-three-and-four-or-more
and-one-and-two-and-three-and-dropped it. Shit! –
I was haunted by the trivial game.

I dreamt eidetic dreams
of catching, dropping, never catching up.

I went to work like an automaton
until the mechanism failed.

Now when time's running out I have more time –
more blank pages in my diaries –
than I know how to use.

I'm not accountable. I forget the date.
I think in Fahrenheit,
ounces, miles, half-pints and twelve-hour clocks.

What's past is prologue to everything I write.
Tomorrow is stuffed full with yesterdays.
Innocence ends when memory begins.

I'm not an honest man.
These lines are comedy; not funny, but comedy.

I've had a life. I'm playing extra time.

This bright December morning is afterwards.

Plan B

If I live long enough –
and I've already had a life –
my brain will decompose.

I once had millions
millions more than I could count
even when I could count.

How many more can I forget
and still know who I am?

I have an exit plan
and if it works
I'll go before my absentmindedness
is absence of a mind.

Odds and arteries are narrowing:
at a blue-bolt stroke
the plan and I could be inoperable.

A defecating simpleton
invalidates the vow.

Plan B is DNR.
I've had a life. Do not resuscitate.

To Be a Pilgrim

Pilgrimage begins in discontent:
you move house but you never feel at home;
you can't enjoy the person you've become.
Could godforsakenness be your complaint?

To be a pilgrim you needn't be devout
or virtuous, and you needn't travel far.
But pilgrims must lose track of where they are
and who they were. A pilgrim travels in doubt.

You may never hear God's angels sing:
God's best at silence and catastrophe.
Hymns? Psalms? Yes. Hum along and make your way
alone, without a father or a king.

Not guilty and not innocent, in retreat
you travel like the naked fugitive
in last night's dream. Cover yourself, forgive
yourself. You think your pilgrimage complete?

A pilgrim's never cured of the complaint.
When symptoms fade you fear the cause is lost.
You want the healing fever of your ghost.
Pilgrimage can end in discontent.

Holiday Inn

Late one evening in the middle of March
I stood beneath the entrance canopy
of a Holiday Inn. We weren't on holiday;
we'd come back north house-hunting for a place
where we could begin the beginning of the end.

Standing there I sensed a stir
that lolloped-stopped-lolloped – and turned into a hare.

And then in April ... Was it the same hare?
I was stargazing through blue tobacco smoke
and the grey vapour of my breath
when a movement brought me down to earth:
a silhouette with that lolloping, stop-start gait.

The Holiday Inn and the buildings round about
and the tarred car parks and a maze of roads –
there are no footpaths –
all this was pastureland five years ago
when we moved south to a house in Gloucestershire.

In the dark the solitary hare
might have been the creature's wraith
come back to sniff out hares' lost thoroughfares.

You Are Here

Blue lochs, green plains and tawny contour lines –
through colour-coded iconicities
I read the landscape and the mind
of an anonymous cartographer.

A smidgen on the map, inch-to-a-mile,
is nothing like Loch Venachar:
brain's blue neurons
make a loch-like locus in my head.

I see the stream of time
in a free-flowing motionless thin line:
a still life watercolour comes alive
and the River Forth meanders over the Carse.

The flat-page map grows three-dimensional.
I'm overshadowed by Ben Ledi:
the cartographer's trigonometry
gives me eagle-sight, a head for heights
and a god's-eye view.

The cartographer reads the landscape of my mind.

Rootstocks

When we came north again we bought this house
because we knew it would keep its promises,
and the garden was a wild entanglement.

Rowan, elder, hazel, oak and birch –
all through May and halfway into June
I watched leaves' lemon-greenery deepening
through shades too subtle-coloured for poetry.

The garden's wide and the ladder's long enough
for full-size trees
but they might take more years than I have left
before they reached their natural fruiting height.
And so the trees we planted – apple, pear
and plum – were grafted onto dwarf rootstocks.

Since mid-December – I write these lines in March –
we've had sub-zero temperatures most nights
and yet fruit buds are filling out.
The garden like the house has promises.

If frost in May aborts the blossoming
I'll pray to the fruitless dwarves
and the native trees to grant me another year.

Eclipse

A solar flare,
infinitesimal cosmic incident,
re-aligned earth's angle to the sun.

The planet slanted
to a new equator and new magnetic poles.
Ice melted in an oceanic thaw
that sank Atlantis
and lapped the summit of Mount Ararat

Land masses floated off as continents.

The last ground-nesting pterodactyls drowned.

Tropical forests lie fossilized beneath Antarctica.

      *   *   *

A loosely woven wall of absent light
spans the Carse.
A cloud absorbs the horizon and the sky.
The land is darker than the last eclipse.

Night is falling on my morning house.
Distances close down.

A field away
a heron stands on the edge of morning night.
A season's rainfall in a week,
a month's in a day.

Darkness gains ground. The heron vanishes.

Seasons

When I was a child the seasons followed rules. Now they frolic through the calendar.

Frogs coupled in the pond in February.

The dashboard sensor showed twenty-four degrees in April in a car park in Dunkeld. In Stirling in July it was fourteen.

Gales sand-blasted the Isle of Mull in June. *The Princess* dragged her anchor in the Sound.

In November raspberries were still ripening on the cane and dwarf daffodils had a second flowering.

* * *

The first snow fell in mid-December at night. Gritting lorries scattered salt and splashed their whirling sunburst flares along Causewayhead. Lit from below, snowflakes were feathered gold.

The coldest December for twenty years. Motorways were blocked by abandoned cars. Days of snow. Days and weeks of snow. Old women slipped and fell and broke their wrists. The coldest snowiest January for twenty ... thirty ... forty ... fifty years.

Schools closed and children learned the meaning of snow.

I sit here gloating in mid-February. Snow is falling again. For the first time in fifty years winter might fill its season. I want an overspill. I want more snow. I bask in the gritting lorries' orange light. The child in me cries 'Again! Again! Again!'

WINTER'S TALES
for Peter and Amanda Carpenter

I'm caught off guard again by winter's tales.

The slenderness of a December dawn
is a healing bruise of yellow-purple-pink.

My boots are trampling out the blackbirds' tracks.
I hear a squeaking, snorting, grunting crunch
from layers of snow that fell on different days.

A flock of waxwings stripped the holly bush.

On the far side of the River Forth
leafless sycamore trees are blossoming
in a crystalline florescence of hoar-frost.

I'm dazzled by the level of the sun.
The ebb is imperceptible ...
I feel uneasy in the sudden dark.

Winter Lines

From the wing mirror to the nearside wing
the filament of spider silk that spanned
the little gap was so thin-spun a strand
it could have been an eyelash glistening
in the dazzle of mid-winter sun.
I knew the thread would snap on our next run.

The sun had set when we got back at four
and in the early dark I didn't think
of searching for a flimsy spider link
between the mirror and the passenger door.

Next morning when I looked the thread was there,
furred with hoar-frost in the freezing air.

A little length of fibre, a spider line
has greater tensile strength than lines of mine.

Stubble Fields

On Sunday mornings we drove to Airthrey Care.
Main roads were gritted;
side-streets and country lanes were paved with ice
from mid-December to the end of February.

We saw flocks – too hazy far-away
to say if they were Greylag or Barnacle –
gleaning Carseland stubble fields.

A thaw lasted a day or half a day:
what pickings did they find
among the bristle-stems of barley and oats?

Months of snow on snow and deep-down frost
made gardening impossible.
I looked for the whiter white of snowdrop tips.

Geese can't go back to their northern breeding grounds
until the steepening angle of the sun
fires the migrant neurons in their brains.

Carseland farmers can't afford to wait:
six-coultered ploughs
turn the frozen stubble fields to loam.

In late February
 the planet tilts a few degrees.
Geese rise in gaggling unison from the Carse:
great wavering skeins are heading north.

Sightings

In Gloucestershire and now in Stirlingshire
year by year I saw fewer swallows and swifts.
Britain's wet summers? Sub-Saharan drought?

I can't recall the occasion for the lunch
or what I ate
but I saw swallows, more than I'd seen for years,
skimming the lawns around Powfoulis House.

And far above my head,
just within range of my Siemens microchips,
I heard the shrill black hunting cries of swifts.

Swallows and swifts criss-crossed and doubled back,
too fast to count, too many and too fast
to follow any bird's trajectory.

On Stirling Bridge

The Forth is tidal up to Stirling Bridge.
The river runs upstream
on a North-Sea surge,
earth and moon
in interplanetary gravitational play.

A Securicor van
on its way to Cornton Vale
turns left at the traffic lights.

Strip-searched and then watched by cctv
some women –
shoplifters, heroin prostitutes,
mothers whose mothers knew no mothering –
still find ways to kill themselves.

Between tides
a man in waders throws a grappling hook
and hauls out shopping trolleys.

On a Minor Road

Driving along B826 we see
proof of a young man's immortality:
a bunch of flowers tied to a scarred tree.

                *　*　*

The key unlocks a simultaneous self.
Neurons fire. New networks fill the brain.
Sensation, cognition are instantaneous:
feet, wrists, palms, fingertips
and the dilating pupils of his eyes.

Not networks in the brain – the brain in them.

The simultaneous self is in control
and sees with a nocturnal clarity,
eyes casting a converging twin-track flight
path on a minor road on a moonless night.

There's no horizon, no sky and no stars.

A voice is echoing the coital moan
of tyres on tarmac. And the engine whines
like an angel entering earth's atmosphere.

The way ahead is clear.

The road unravelling from the pool of light
is travelling faster than the speed of sight.

Rough Gardening

A glance encompasses the task
but fumbling thumbs and an arthritic hip
make the work last longer than I thought.
Or didn't think.

Rough gardening begins where reason ends.
I hear the delta waves
of my oceanic ignorance
lapping the tidal islands in my brain.

Rooting out winter moss with a spring-tine rake
I grunt 'One and two and three and four'
along each swathe of the lawn.

Grunting faster to keep pace with my breath
I lose the rhythm of the line.
I wheeze and hawk up gobs of nightshift phlegm.

I take a smoker's break
and re-engage the frontals of my mind.

I've learned – lost-learned – hands-on allegiances
and now I'm learning to be old
here on this half-acre of the Carse.

I remember when unfinished things
taunted me and wouldn't let me sleep.

Now I can stop before the task's complete,
down tools and still have the blessing of an ache
as rare as innocence but less dangerous.

I stroke catmint and sniff my fingertips.

Carseland Diary

Every morning for a week – ten days? I should keep a diary. A scrim of white-frilled ice covered the pond.

I should keep a diary of snowdrops, crocuses, aconites, daffodils, hazel catkins and hellebores. I chant the names when no one is listening.

I celebrate the little festival of light around the middle of February when the Carse tilts to catch the steeper angle of the sun.

In March the water level in the pond was as high as the stepping stones. March was a hot dry month on the Carse last year.

The pear was the first fruit tree to flower this year. I should keep a diary. Ground-frost is air-frost on the lower levels of the Carse. White petals blackened overnight.

I felt no warmth in the April sun. I raised my right hand in reflex salute to shade my eyes from the glare and dry my tears. The sky was blue and imperturbable.

I should note the date of the first honey-bee – a single bee or one bee at a time? – to nuzzle the pieris flowers' white cluster-bells. Perhaps bees waggle-dance only when catmint blossom-time begins.

The soil in May was too cold for seeds to germinate and yet fruit-buds were swelling on apple trees, plum trees, gooseberry bushes and raspberry canes; half-promise of a daze of harvesting. I chant the names when no one is listening.

I should keep records of the weights of fruits and the plucking days from July to November. But not in leaner years when measuring would be discourteous.

I should note the date of the first incoming skein of greylag geese, and the final mowing of the half-moon lawn.

Anthem

In my disorder I shivered sweated, yawned
with fear and wrote some lines that went beyond
wit's end. We travelled south. We hadn't planned
on coming north again and buying this land
of little things where dwarf ferns unfurl their fronds,
newts and frogs come back to the garden pond,
a mistle thrush sings before the day has dawned.

Yes – any how-when-where by drop-dead chance.
And so I've been rehearsing final things
for years. I've bought my ashes in advance.
Until that harvesting
I'll observe the natural ordinance
of fern and newt and frog and a thrush that sings
the anthem in my land of little things.

ORCHARD
for Cara

Ignorance or bloody-mindedness?
Someone in Planning wrote to say the plot
was still scheduled as Agricultural Land.

Your cottage had been a small-farm dairy.
The patch of land you bought
was a half-acre unplanned wilderness.

The seller, the old farmer, must have known
that just below the inch-thick layer of soil
the site was a midden, a tip. We filled a skip
with solid, hard-fired indiarubber tyres,
shards of terracotta tiles or pots,
lumps of mortar, half-bricks, builder's rubble,
shattered cast-iron gutters, a rusted coil
of fence wire, boulder stones, animal bones
and bluish-grey boot-clogging Cotswold clay.

That land was never arable.

We worked the land until we made a loam.
We sowed lawn seed and then we planted trees,
apple, pear and plum, not to appease
officialdom nor as a compromise –
sylviculture on agricultural land –
but for blossoming, fruit and the trance of harvesting.

PASSWORDS
for Nick

When you come back
you tell me of the world I lived in once.
I couldn't live there now:
new microelectronic gadgetry,
new laws and passwords, bigger labyrinths.

You signed the Act. I guess at what you do:
intercept ethereal messages
and gather secret knowledge of secret worlds,
spectral intelligence of life and death.

Off duty you investigate Culdees
and other clients of God: kings, warriors, saints.
You decipher stones and manuscripts
in Latin, Anglo-Saxon, ogham, runes.

I read your reading of dead languages:
lost worlds are translated back to life.

When you leave you go so far away
I couldn't follow even if I tried.

I wish you now the uncensored gift of time.

Orbit

Whatever I'm doing – gathering fallen leaves,
writing in longhand, cursing Microsoft –
as soon as I stop, sit back or straighten up
I hear the tinnient hiss in my deaf ear.
And then – the thought thinks me – I think of you.

You have a time-free covenant with time:
you always look years younger than you are.
You age so slowly I see no difference
between last year and this, our fiftieth.

You know all you want to know about me.
There isn't much: grass, trees, rough gardening
and poetry. No profitable skills.

I'm deaf, incompetent. I find myself
in elliptical orbit around you.

Any fool can fall in love. The test
is to keep loving long after the fall.

Some things change: I look at you and see
new strangeness, new familiarity.

Motorway

Cars, vans, lorries big as bungalows.
Torrential rain and back-spray: we're monsooned.
The road ahead is just fifty metres long.
Air bags? Braking distances?

How can creatures breathe in that drowning world?

You switch the wipers to their fastest beat
and yet the windscreen's an hour-long snare-drum roll.

The sun breaks through at two in the afternoon.
Tarmac steams in opalescent light.

We flip the visors down against the dazzle.
On long straights I can see the vanishing point
that never vanishes, or hasn't vanished yet.

Melodies, jingles, fragments, single notes –
My brain's off-watch; I know you'll find the way.

Husbandries

Our half-acre of the Carse
is big enough for different husbandries.

You dead-head roses and make new roses bloom.
You prune hard and trees grow shapelier.

Seven years and I'm still digging out
boulders and the sunken stumps of shrubs,
still pleaching holly laterals to thicken the hedge.

You transplant irises, fuchsia, lilac, sage
and propagate new properties of light.

In full foliage the garden's dense
and even in bare winter it's big enough
for games of find-the-other-gardener.

You never hide
but there are times when I lose sight of you.

When I call 'Yoo-hoo?' and say your name,
you call back to me, 'Yes. Here I am'.

Sounds enter my brain
through a microchip in my left ear.
When left's not right I don't know where you are
or where I am.

This is our sixth garden.
Somewhere along the way from Stirlingshire
to Gloucestershire and back again
we lost our forever letters. No great loss:
forever is however long love lasts.

Winter Wrens

I lose a box of matches, a paper-knife,
a Vicks inhaler nasal stick, two pens
and a roofer's business card beneath the layers
of paper on my desk.

Coffee ... Kitchen window ... I watch my wife
scattering bacon-fat scraps beneath the hedge
of beech and holly – too low for the see-and-fetch
of crows and magpies – for the winter wrens.

I've outlived myself by twenty years
and I've grown grotesque
sitting at this desk in afterlife
composing, decomposing godless prayers.

'My wife'. I write the words, 'my wife', again –
And you're not mine. You're the one who cares
for flowers and shrubs and wrens in this garden.

I steal another day. I am a thief.
Through my clouding lens
and the forgetfulness that comes with age
I loosen loyalties. I lose old friends.
I ignore the unnatural world's affairs.

I practise my belief
in you, us, gardens, words and winter wrens.

www.ingramcontent.com/pod-product-compliance
Lightning Source LLC
Chambersburg PA
CBHW042119100526
44587CB00025B/4115